D. R.
Caranoc.

Prayers and Graces

And I said to the man who stood at the gate of the year:
'Give me a light, that I may tread safely into the unknown'
And he replied: 'Go out into the darkness and put your hand
into the hand of God. That shall be to you better than light
And safer than a known way.'

M. Louise Haskins

In memory of Jessie Jones

Prayers and Graces

Collected by Michael Jones

Floris Books

First published in 1980 by Floris Books
Revised and enlarged 1987
© Floris Books, 1980, 1987

British Library CIP Data

Prayers and graces.
1. Prayer-books
I. Jones, Michael, *date*
242'.8   BV245

ISBN 0–86315–063–2

Printed in Great Britain at
The Camelot Press Ltd, Southampton

Contents

Foreword

Prayer and meditation are complementary activities. They are both aspects of an inner activity and need to be sharply differentiated before we can see how they flow together in practice. Various forms of meditational exercises are available today and if pursued with sufficient dedication they will have a powerful effect. If this is to be beneficial in the long term such exercises must be balanced to avoid either a self-enclosed hardening of the soul or a dreamy nervousness that cannot face the world objectively.

Basically meditation is a path of spiritual development, a reaching into higher worlds. Carefully chosen objects, feelings and ideas or a sequence of ideas are made the sole content of consciousness for a certain period of time. Their true essence then begins to penetrate the human soul and a kind of well is built into the depths, making contact with different levels of reality possible.

But the ability to live in different realms of consciousness and on different planes does not necessarily mean that we form a living connection with the divine. In order to progress in our meditations we must develop a strong centre within ourselves, but this must not blind us to the presence of Christ. The being of Christ is creative on all levels of existence, including the physical world, and works always for the enduring good of *all* beings. A relationship with Christ is possible on all levels and can be stimulated by allowing passages from the

7

Gospels to resound¹ within us. It is this connection with something divine outside ourselves which at the same time freely penetrates the ego, that is the content of what we call prayer.

Many of the verses here will be found to have the character of a kind of affirmation. This is particularly so of the verses of Rudolf Steiner for children and adults. Through a sincere use of these an affirmative level is reached in the human will. It is from this level that prayer can arise. They help to strengthen the weak inner life of modern man, who lacks the strength to pray honestly.

The verses for children included here should not be taught especially, but be spoken by an adult for the child. Gradually the child will grow to know them with his whole being.

Prayer and meditation should always be taken up with absolute freedom. Nowhere is this more important than in praying for the dead. The dead experience the inner landscape of the human soul left behind on earth. The relationship between a verse and one's own inner perceptions and memories should be completely natural.

I hope this anthology will be of help to everyone embarked on the lifelong task of learning to pray.

Michael Jones

Introduction

Can we grow again into an effective practice of prayer? There are many obstacles in the way. For many, it is very difficult to believe in any being who might hear our prayer. We look out into the vast and complex universe, which appears indifferent to us; and looking into ourselves, we see so much egoism and triviality. 'If there be a spirit behind all this immensity — how could this spirit be in any way concerned with what goes on in our minds? How could we conceivably pray anything that would be worth his hearing?' Some such feeling as this holds back many from prayer today: and the advocates of prayer often strengthen this feeling in others, when their claims of success through prayer show obvious marks of great unconscious selfishness. Those who hear such claims may easily feel: 'Well, to a being who could not see through So-and-so, we would not *want* to pray!' Yet to be able to pray is the greatest enrichment of human life. Is there any way of approaching prayer on which we could begin to throw off the hindrances of our selfishness and triviality, and the unbelief which is ultimately their consequence?

There are certain deep moods of soul, described from a particular point of view by Rudolf Steiner, which mean a great deal for the regeneration of prayer. They form together a foundation on which prayer can be built. The first begins when we see truly the far-reaching effects we are continually having on the world around us. The egoist in us whispers, 'You don't mean anything to

9

anyone' (perhaps varying this with 'You mean every-thing to *someone*') but in fact, the effects of our lives are continually flowing out, helping or harming thousands of other lives. This is true however limited our sphere of action may appear. From a hospital bed, a lonely cottage, a prison cell — or from a life in the strictest routine between barren office work and the crushing loneliness that a city can sometimes offer — innumerable effects pass into the general life of humanity. No one can measure the effects of his own actions. What you did ten years ago is having effects today in parts of the world you have never visited, among people of whom you know nothing; and what we did *not* do that could have been done — this too is having its effects.

All this can become a mood 'I am connected with all the world', and we can extend this to our thoughts and feelings, as well as our actions. Against each one of us are aimed, as against the woman taken in adultery and brought to Jesus, the stony criticisms of others. But what matters far more is that Christ writes the truth of what we are: the effects of all that lives in our soul, into the substance of the earth.

When we realize this steadily, our angel comes nearer to us; and into the earnestness of this mood can come a second realization, through which our memory of the past grows warmer. We can see how great the wisdom is which works through all that destiny has brought to us — in the events which were not of our making within this life, which came to us as gifts from the world. And of many things, both successes and misfortunes, that seem at first as if they were due to ourselves, we may come to feel, 'What I really did myself to bring these things about is less important — these joys and these sorrows were really brought to me by a wise destiny'. As the means for these experiences, we can begin to thank the great shining ring of the senses; and for their interpretation all we have received from the riches of living thought. So we can feel ourselves as among the multitude to whom the Christ gives loaves and fishes, for through our senses we receive nourishment, and in our thinking life we are fed from the world-ocean. In thankfulness for these gifts our whole being is refreshed; while in thankless receiving, our whole humanity dies. When we have really felt this, the universe no longer looks so indifferent. We begin to see that it is possible for a mighty power to be lovingly concerned with the needs of many lesser beings. We only forget this because gratitude has to some extent dried up in us under the influence of a mechanical conception of the world.

These two moods of the soul — community with the world, and gratitude — can be very much strengthened by participation in the Act of Consecration of Man, the communion service of The Christian Community. They live in all that is said and done; but they are expressed particularly at the beginning of the Offering. We are doubly debtors to the Spirit; for we have done harm, and are liable for damages; and we have received in abundance without payment. And as we meet the steady forgiveness of the Father, there is born the impulse — not to pay back in full, which is impossible — but to bring the kind of offering of which we are capable, and which can be brought in completest freedom. The angel has drawn near to us — and now we walk at his side, and look into the future.

More than at any previous time in the history of the world, is the gaze of human beings into the future troubled by fear and anxiety. Neither the condition of our personal lives, nor of humanity in general, seems to give ground for confidence. A great deal is done in order to drug our fears into silence; but it is better to face them, and learn from them. The sense of gratitude for the wisdom of destiny in the past, which we have tried to develop, will help us; but we need a new inner deed. All the goodness and greatness we have been able to find in the world — recognizing the works of creation, and the deeds of guidance, by the spiritual beings in the service of God, and the fundamental longing for love and justice that is in all this, *and more*, is to be found in the future too. 'And greater works than these will they do.'

Greater than the good we have known, is the good which is to come about through the work of God in man. It is not a question of vague general hope, but of the enkindling of a practical will towards a divine 'magic', which working through us will redeem evil; and of believing that we shall meet this same practical will, often in much greater degree, in others. Just where the greatest evils are met — as they were among the men and women in the concentration camps, or in Hiroshima and Nagasaki, for example — grounds for confidence in human beings can be found. It is sometimes more difficult in day-to-day dealings, or when we watch tragically unnecessary quarrels, but they are to be found here too, if we look closely enough.

When we attend the Act of Consecration we have in the third part the opportunity to observe the power, that is in a true sense magical, of Christ to transmute and to unite. All through Nature this power is foreshadowed; here it is revealed; and we begin to see how in general, prayer can *work*; how it is akin to all that in nature helps the organism to control and order earthly substances, to bring them into the service of life. Praying in Christ's 'name', in mindfulness of his purpose, we increase — because he waits for free human co-operation — the powers that are at his disposal. Walking with our angel, we come into the circle of the mighty beings of the hierarchies who serve his redeeming love.

There is still a fourth quality that we need as a foundation for the life of prayer; it can be described as the spirit of youth — the readiness to receive and to have joy in the unexpected, and to look at the familiar with wonder. Where the Christ is, we grow young. The ages of experience behind us shrink into a brief preparation for the real work that is to come. Only if we are able to forget, as well as to remember, can we hear the new things that are being said to us when we pray. For prayer is a conversation, in which one party is unfortunately inclined, owing to deafness perhaps, to do all the talking. It is only the child in us who really wants, and is able, to listen. But if each morning, along with our sense of belonging to the world, our gratitude for all that is given, and our confidence, we can feel readiness to meet the unknown sustained in us by joy — then we shall read the events that come as true messages, and hear within ourselves, clothed it may be in familiar or it may be in unfamiliar words, the living Word.

The whole of the Act of Consecration is rightly felt as a source of joy; but it is above all in receiving the Cup that we unite ourselves with the source of joy and youth: 'I am the true vine'. This is a joy which forgets only what is rightly forgotten — not the needs of others, but the stupidities and weaknesses of the past that otherwise hinder us. Now into our own keeping the angel gives us the star, which has shone over all our life; the star which is itself one jewel in the robe of the sun. That both the sun and star may shine in us on earth in our peace.

Through the course of the year are woven the four qualities which are the groundwork of prayer. At midsummer we can heed the voice that tells us of the guilt woven by man into the earth. In the depth of winter there can glow in us thankfulness for the Christmas mystery of the incarnation. In autumn Michael's battle with the dragon gives the great example of confidence over fear. And in spring the power of the resurrection quickens joy. We are slow pupils indeed, but the Spirit of the Year is a patient teacher; and in the Act of Consecration of Man, he leads us into his inner room.

Adam Bittleston

Prayers for Children

For expectant mothers

Light and warmth
Of the divine spirit world
Envelop me.

Before the birth

And the soul of the child
Be given to me
According to your will
Out of the worlds of spirit.

After the birth

And the soul of the child
Be guided by me
According to your will
Into the worlds of spirit.

Rudolf Steiner

Prayer for small children spoken by a grown-up

Light may stream into your being,
Light that can dwell within you;
With my love and my warmth
I unite with its rays.
I think my best thoughts of joy
On the stirrings in your heart.
    They shall strengthen you,
    They shall carry you,
    They shall enlighten you.
I wish to gather up my glad thoughts
    Before the steps of your life
That they may unite with your will to live
That this will may find strength in itself
In all the world
More and more
Through its very own self.

Rudolf Steiner

Morning Prayer

What makes the plant blossom?
    It is God's wisdom.
What makes man alive?
    It is God's love.
What makes the sun circle?
    It is God's might.
What makes the clouds wander?
    It is God's will.

And thus may live in my heart:
    God's wisdom
    God's love
    God's might and
    God's will.
So that I become:
    thoughtful
    loving
    strong and
    good.

Rudolf Steiner

Evening Prayer

In the darkness of night
  My thoughts
  My wishes
  My deeds
Stream forth.

May God receive them.
May he transform them
  With his wisdom
  With his love and
  With his strength,
So that I may be with him,
And in the morning
Awaken with his blessing.

Aletta Adler

Evening Prayers

Angels of light are bearing me
Into the Spirit's house —

Rudolf Steiner

You rest in the Divine of the world
You will find yourself in the Divine of the world.

Rudolf Steiner

Thou Angel of God, my Guardian dear,
To whom God's love commits me here:
Even this night be at my side —
To light, to guard, to watch, to guide.

Origin unknown

Soul-Shrine

Thou angel of God who hast charge of me
From the fragrant father of mercifulness,
The gentle encompassing of the Sacred Heart
To make round my soul-shrine this night,
    Oh, round my soul-shrine this night.

Ward from me every distress and danger,
Encompass my course over the ocean of truth,
I pray thee, place thy pure light before me,
O bright beauteous angel on this very night.
    Bright beauteous angel on this very night.

Be thyself the guiding star above me,
Illume thou to me every reef and shoal,
Pilot my barque on the crest of the wave,
To the restful haven of the waveless sea.
    Oh, the restful haven of the waveless sea.

Alexander Carmichael

Evening Prayer

Matthew, Mark, Luke, and John,
Bless the bed that I lie on.
Four corners to my bed,
Four angels round my head;
One to watch and one to pray
And two to bear my soul away.

Traditional

The Four Archangels

In the Name of God the Almighty
To my right Michael
And to my left Gabriel
And before me Uriel
And behind me Raphael
And over my head
The presence of God.

Ancient Jewish

Evening Prayer

From my head to my feet
I am the image of God.
From my heart to my hands
I feel the breath of God.
When I speak with my mouth
I will follow God's will.
When I see God
In Father and Mother,
In all dear people,
In animal and flower,
In tree and stone,
No fear shall I feel
But love will fill me
For everything around me.

Rudolf Steiner

Morning Prayer

Sun, you shine above my head,
Stars, you shine above fields and cities,
Animals, you stir upon the earth-mother,
Plants, you live through powers of earth and sun,
Stones, you make firm animal and plant
And me, the human being,
In whom God's might
Lives in head and heart,
Who walks with God's power
Throughout the world.

Rudolf Steiner

Evening Prayer

My heart thanks
That my eye can see
That my ear can hear
That I can wakefully feel
In Mother and Father
In all dear people
In stars and clouds:
 God's light
 God's love
 God's being
Which, sleeping,
 Beaming
 Loving
Grace-giving, protect me.

Rudolf Steiner

Evening Prayer for Advent and Christmas

Now the hours of dark are long
And the days are short and cold.
Mary lays her gentle hands
On the sleeping heads of men,
And she sings her songs of joy
Softly through the winter world.
May her Son be in our hearts,
His golden light upon our way.

Adam Bittleston

Prayer

For children over nine years old

When I see the sun,
I think God's spirit.
When I use my hand,
God's soul lives in me.
When I take a step,
God's will walks in me.
And when I see other people,
God's soul lives in them.
And so it lives, too,
In beast and plant and stone.
Fear can never reach me
When I think God's spirit,
When I live God's soul,
When I walk in God's will.

Rudolf Steiner

Morning Prayer

The sun sends forth
To earth its light;
God's spirit gleams
In sunshine bright.
The plants all drink
The light of sun,
And so they grow
On the field and hill
As work of God.
Man too bears God
In heart and soul,
Thro' the spirit of God.
I love God's spirit
In hearts and hands,
In sun and moon

Rudolf Steiner

Morning Prayer

Above me stands the sun,
It gives me loving light;
In the light, God give to me
The noble power of life,
And the power of God,
It rays out everywhere,
In every stone,
In all the plants,
In animal and in man;
And when the power of love
Is living in my heart too
Then comes the power of God
Into my Self as well —
The higher power of God
Is gift from Christ
To man on earth.

Rudolf Steiner

Song

The sun's light floods
Through widths of space,
The birds' song rings
Through heights of air;
The gracious plants
Spring up on earth;
And human souls
Lift up their thanks
To spirits of the world.

Rudolf Steiner

The sun gives light
To the plants,
For the sun
Loves the plants.
So one man gives soul-light
To others
When he loves them.

Rudolf Steiner

Morning Prayers

The eye of man is filled with joy
By the shining light of the sun.
Thus the soul is also filled with joy
By the spirit of God that lives in everything
As the invisible Sun
Who shines in love upon all beings.

Rudolf Steiner

My thoughts are flying to school:
There will my body be formed
For right activity,
There will my soul be guided
In right powers of life,
There will my spirit be awakened
To right human Being.

Rudolf Steiner

The sun sends forth
To earth its light.
God's spirit gleams
In sunshine bright.
The plants all drink
The light of sun,
And so they grow
On field and meadow,
Belovéd children
Of the spirit of God —
All men do bear
In heart and soul
God's spirit too;
And in their hands
God's spirit works;
I love the spirit of God
Because He lives in me.

Rudolf Steiner

Evening Prayer

To wonder at beauty
Stand guard over truth
Look up to the noble,
Resolve on the good:
This leadeth man truly
To purpose in living
To right in his doing
To peace in his feeling
To light in his thinking,
And teaches him trust,
In the working of God,
In all that there is
In the widths of the world,
In the depth of the soul.

Rudolf Steiner

Canticle to the Sun

Praised be God for brother Sun,
Who shines with splendid glow,
He brings the golden day to us,
Thy glory does he show!

Praised be God for sister Moon
And every twinkling star;
They shine in heaven most bright and clear,
All glorious they are.

Praised be God for brother Wind
That storms across the skies,
And then grows still, and silent moves,
And sweetly sings and sighs.

Praised be God for Water pure,
Her usefulness we tell,
So humble, precious, clean and good,
She works for us so well.

Praised be God for brother Fire
Friendly and wild and tame,
Tender and warm, mighty and strong,
A flashing, flaring flame.

Praised be God for mother Earth,
Who keeps us safe and well,
Whose mother heart all warm with love
Dark in her depths doth dwell.

St Francis

May wisdom shine through me
May love glow in me
May strength penetrate me
That in me may arise
A helper of mankind
A servant of holy things,
Selfless, and true.

Origin unknown

I look into the world of stars—
I understand their splendour
If I can behold in it
God's wisdom guiding the world.
I look into my own heart
I understand my heart's beat,
If I can feel within it
God's goodness guiding men.
I understand nothing of the starry splendour,
And nothing of the beat of my heart,
If I see not, and feel not, God.
God has led my soul
Into this life,
And He will lead me to ever new life:
So say all who can rightly think.
And every further year we live,
Speaks more of God and the soul everlasting.

Rudolf Steiner

Graces

Earth who gave to us this food:
Sun who made it ripe and good:
Dear Sun
Dear Earth
By you we live,
To you our loving thanks we give.

Christian Morgenstern

Earth, sun and air
Have wrought by God's care
That the plants live and bear.
Praising God for this food,
In Truth live we would
Bearing Beauty and Good.

Origin unknown

Before the flour the mill
Before the mill the grain,
The sun, the earth, the rain
The beauty of God's will.

Origin unknown

We thank the water, earth and air
And all the helping powers they bear.
We thank the people— loving, good,
Who grow and cook our daily food.
And now at last we thank the sun,
The light and life for everyone.

Origin unknown.

The food we eat
The lives we weave
Come from God
We give thanks.

Michael Motteram

Blessed art Thou, O Lord our God,
King of the Universe,
Who bringeth forth bread from the earth.

Ancient Jewish

Substance of Earth,
Essence of Light,
Grace of Heaven:
In us unite.

L. Francis Edmunds

The light has formed our food for earth
And speech has formed the souls of men.
Eternal Light, eternal Word
Within our hearts be seen, be heard.

Adam Bittleston

Let us receive
With gratitude and in peace
The gracious and loving gifts
        Of the earth
And those who labour on the earth,
        Of the heavens
And those who rule the heavens.

Richard Hope

For food and fellowship
And all the love and beauty
And bounty of heaven and earth
        We give thanks.

Will Sawkins

Pressed from brown earth, O seed
In God's warm light thou ripenest.
 Blessed with his fullness, too,
 Awake, O heart!
In gratitude to Him
Who gives increase
And bids us live.

Origin unknown

For the deep earth that cradles the seed
For the rain that brings forth the green leaves
For the stars that give form to the flowers
For the warm sun that ripens the fruit:
 For all this goodness and beauty
 Our heavenly Father, we thank Thee.

Gladys Hahn

We break this bread together
With thankful hearts aware
Not bread alone —
But God's Life and Love
We share.

Angelus Silesius

The peace of Christ
Be upon each thing our eye takes in:
Upon each thing our mouth takes in:
Upon our body which is of earth:
Upon our body which is of God.

Origin unknown

Bread comes from grain
And grain from light
And light from God
All pure and bright.
In fruits of earth
God's glory shines
Fill Thou our hearts
O Lord Divine.

Martin Tittmann

Fruits of earth
Gifts of Heaven,
In deeds of sacrifice
To mankind given,
In peace received
A healing leaven.

Origin unknown

This food which we are about to eat
Is Thy gift, O God,
And the fruit of the labour of many beings.
We are grateful for it and bless it,
May it give us health and strength and life
And may it increase our love.

Origin unknown

After a meal

The cup of my body
Has received your grace,
O Lord.
May it shine,
May it ray forth
Your grace
Into the world

Heinrich Heine

The plant roots quicken in the night of the earth,
The leaves unfold through the might of the air,
The fruit grows ripe through the power of the sun

So quickens the soul in the shrine of the heart,
And man's spirit unfolds in the light of the world,
So ripens man's strength in the glory of God.

And root and leaf and the ripe fruit's blessing
Support the life of men on earth;
And soul and spirit upward pressing
May raise themselves in thanks to God.
      Amen.

Rudolf Steiner

The plants burst forth
From the soil of the earth,
Rain pours down
From the night of the sky;
And love bursts forth
In the heart of Man
And wisdom pours down
Into our human spirit.

Rudolf Steiner

In root and leaf,
In flower and seed,
Upon Christ's Body
Do I feed.
Christ be in head,
In heart, in limb;
In thought, word, deed,
Not I, but Him.

Isobel Wyatt

With every bite of bread
Think of the sun shining red.
The sun-orb warms the tiny seeds
And lets them grow as loving deeds.
With every bite of bread
Thy brother's need bestead
Who lonely, only on hunger feeds.
May I, whom God gave blessing deeds,
Give bread and love for my brother's needs.

Herbert Hahn

Graces for Simple Meals

Bread of Earth
And Bread of Heaven
Unto us by Thee are given.
For these Thy gifts we raise our hearts
In thankfulness
And in joy.

John Hunter

'Tis not the bread that nourishes
What heals us in the bread
Is God's eternal Word,
His Spirit and his Life indeed

Angelus Silesius

Illness and Death

Prayer for a Sick Child

Eternal Father, Thy care and Thy blessing
Have held and warmed us all
Since the beginning of worlds,
Grant that this Thy child
Held in Thy care
Warmed by Thy blessing
Receive healing and strength
According to Thy Will
Which works in her/him,
Which works in us.
Beside this child may we see Christ.

The last words may be prayed three times over, as if the thought they contain was living in us, first between the brows and just above the eyes; the second time in the heart; the third time in the hands. Or the prayer may be said once with great earnestness.

Adam Bittleston

For those who are ill:

God's protecting, blessing ray
May it fill my growing soul
So that it may apprehend
Strengthening forces everywhere.
It doth will to pledge itself
To awaken in itself,
Full of life, the might of love
Thus to see the power of God
On the pathway of its life
And to work in God's design
With everything it has.

Rudolf Steiner

God's Spirit, fill thou me
My soul endow with strength
With strength also my heart
My heart that seeketh Thee
Seeketh through deep desire
Through deep desire for health
For health and courage strong
That streams into my limbs
Streams as a noble gift
God's gift from Thee, God's Spirit
God's spirit fill Thou me.

Rudolf Steiner

Illness

Hearts that love, suns that warm
Ye footprints of Christ in the Father's world-all.
We call you out of our own hearts
We seek you in our own spirit
      O strive to him/her.

Rays of the human hearts, warm, mindful, longing,
Ye home-lands of Christ, in the Father's
  house of earth,
We call you out of our own hearts
We seek you in our own spirit
      O live with him/her.

Radiant love of man, warming glow of the sun,
Ye soul-vestments of Christ, in the Father's
  temple of man:
We call you out of our own hearts
We seek you in our own spirit
      O help in him/her.

Rudolf Steiner

This should only be used during a crisis and not by the patient.

53

Spoken by the patient.

I am now surrounded by the pure being of God
And I am steeped in the Holy Spirit of life,
     love and wisdom.
I acknowledge thy, being and thy power,
O Spirit who dost bless.
Blot out now in thy divine wisdom my mortal errors
And bring into being my world
Through the power of love
According to thy perfect law.

Rudolf Steiner

The Good Shepherd lead thee
Where thou art meeting
The tasks of destiny
That thou mayest serve God.

The shining breath of the Spirit
Bear warmth into thy soul,
Granting thee strength for action
In peace with men.

Adam Bittleston

During convalescence:

Have no fear!
Every illness is a gift of destiny.
A time for taking stock of oneself.
Make use of this time.
Have no fear!

Think on this:
He achieves who knows the extent of his capabilities,
But within these limits,
Makes full and regal use of his powers.

Know this also:
Self-restraint strengthens and increases these
    powers,
Enabling them to keep indolence at bay.
Should it prevail
It would destroy the forces of life.
Have no fear!

Rudolf Steiner

Before the Funeral

During the days between death and the funeral the departed ones live in the memories of their life. It is helpful at this time to surround the soul with a feeling of silent devotion. A relative or friend on his own may read aloud from the Gospel of St John. A priest of The Christian Community will be able to give further advice appropriate to the situation. The prayers and meditations which follow and others like them should not be read between death and the funeral.

O Christ I remember, with love and thankfulness,
Those I have known
Who have passed through the gate of death.
I know that some of these have looked on my soul
From the realm in which their souls dwell.
I thank Thee for all I have received from them:
For Thou art Lord of human destiny.
May my meeting again with them
Be blessed by Thy Light.
May my thoughts and feelings reach unto them
        through Thee.
Through Thee may they add warmth and purpose
To my earthly life.

Adam Bittleston

Hear our soul's request
Sent to Thee in deepest trust.
We need here for work on earth
Strength and power from spirit lands
For which we thank dead friends.

Rudolf Steiner

Ye who watch over souls in the spheres,
Ye who work on souls in the spheres,
Ye spirits who, in protection of men's souls,
Work lovingly out of the wisdom of worlds,
Hear our prayers, behold our love
Which would unite
With your helping streaming forces,
Divining spirit,
Radiating love.

Rudolf Steiner

My love will be with thee in spirit realms.
Let thy soul be found
By my seeking soul.
Let thy coldness be soothed,
And soothed thy warmth,
By my thinking of thy Being.
So shall we still be united,
I with thee
And thou with me.

Rudolf Steiner

May my love be woven as an offering
Into the sheaths which now surround you,
Cooling your heat,
Warming your cold,
Live upwards
Borne by love,
Endowed with light.

Rudolf Steiner

May my soul's love
Make its way unto thee
May my love's inmost sense
Make its way unto thee
That they sustain thee
That they enfold thee
In heights of hope
In realms of love.

Rudolf Steiner

Those who have gone
Through the gate of Death
Are gazing at me,
They enliven me,
They are with me;
Their strength is streaming down to me.

Rudolf Steiner

Suicide

May what is true in you
Dear friend
Arise beyond the threshold
Despite the ruins
Of your self-destroyed habitation.
We
Who follow your destiny
Wish to be mindful
That you too are mindful
And standing upright
Look back on the ruins
With the decision
To build them up once more
Into a firm new dwelling

Dora Baker

For a young person who had taken her own life:

Imagine the dead one in a radiance of light

Divine Light shines
Through the Divine Word.

     Rudolf Steiner

May the path of your soul
Draw near to the peace of Christ
May the gaze of your soul
Be lifted to the Spirit
May the longing of your soul
Be settled by God's Life.

     Adam Bittleston

In the weaving of the ether
Man's web of destiny
Is received by Angels, Archangels, Archai.

Into the astral world
The just consequences of man's earthly life
Die into Exousiai, Dynameis, Kyriotetes.

In the essence of their deeds
The honest creations of man's earthly life
Are resurrected in Thrones, Cherubim
        and Seraphim.

Rudolf Steiner

Prayers for
Special Occasions

House Blessing

May soul be living in this house
May this soul be permeated by the Spirit
Who shall seek in the foundation
Firm will,
That in it may grow
The sense of goodness
In all the building's rooms
And that from above
There may unite
The blessing of the Spirit
And the grace of God
In all who dwell therein.

Rudolf Steiner

May he who enters bring love into this place,
May he who stays find knowledge in this house,
May he who goes, take with him from this place
       the gift of peace.

Rudolf Steiner

May this house be founded
On the goodness of the earth.
May the walls of this house be blessed
By the four winds of the heaven.
May the roof of this house be guarded
By heights and the stars above.

So that all who live in this house,
All who seek shelter in this house,
All who strive, protected by this house,
Find hope and strength to live,
Find love and joy to give,
Find faith and meaning in their destiny.

Celtic

Crisis

To turn towards the light
In times of darkest need,
To lift the soul's clear sight
The Spirit-dawn to heed,
The will of man to earthly plane,
This be, and evermore remain.

Rudolf Steiner

*This verse may be used in time of war,
or whenever a country or community
is in difficulty.*

For times of acute crisis

God the Holy
Holy and Mighty
Holy and Immortal
Have mercy on me.

Traditional

Intercessory Prayer

Through thankfulness of heart
Towards the powers of life,
Through thoughts that seek
The Healing Spirit,
May my prayer for . . .
Work in the realm of Christ

Strength
For the fulfilment of that Will
In whose service he entered the earthly body
Be given to his soul.

Light
For the revelation of the Star
Which stood over his earthly birth
Shine in his life.

Peace
In the hearing of the Word
That is spoken to us by Christ
Be for his body's health.

Adam Bittleston

Prayer for the West

I carry my suffering
Into the sinking sun.
I place all my sorrows
Into his shining orb.
Purified by light,
Transformed by love,
They will return
As helpful thoughts,
As strength
For joyful deeds of sacrifice.

Rudolf Steiner

Morning Prayer

O Michael, I commend myself to your protection.
I unite myself with your guidance
With all the strength of my heart,
That this very day today
May mirror the power of your will
In the ordering of my destiny.

Rudolf Steiner

Evening Prayer

Picture the blue orb of the heavens and the great multitude of stars

With wordless reverence
The vision of my soul
Goes into the depths of space
Where it will receive
What pours into my heart:
Light and love and life.

Rudolf Steiner

To Bring Peace

I carry Rest within me,
I bear within myself
Forces giving me strength.
Full will I fill myself
With the warmth of these forces,
I will drench myself
With the power of my will.
And I will feel
How rest outpours itself
Through all my being,
If I strengthen myself
To come upon Rest
As a force within me
Through this my striving's power.

Rudolf Steiner

Against Fear

May the events that seek me
Come unto me;
May I receive them
With a quiet mind
Through the Father's ground of peace
On which we walk.

May the people who seek me
Come unto me;
May I receive them
With an understanding heart
Through the Christ's stream of love
In which we live.

May the spirits who seek me
Come unto me;
May I receive them
With a clear soul
Through the healing Spirit's Light
By which we see.

Adam Bittleston

The Twenty-Third Psalm

The Lord who speaks in my inmost being
Is my shepherd.
I shall not feel any need.
He lets me tarry in the pastures of tender green,
He leads me to the stream of the water of life,
He restores my soul.
He guides me along the way of truthfulness
In the prevailing strength of his own true being.
And even if I walk in the abyss of the dark of death
I have no fear of the threatening evil
For thou art with me.
Thy rod is my support
Thy staff is my comfort.
Before the countenance of my enemies
Thou preparest a table for me
Thou anointest my head with oil
Thou fillest my cup to overflowing.
Yea, goodness and mercy it is
That bears me all my life through,
And in the House of the Lord
Who speaks in my innermost being
Will I dwell ever in peace.

Interpreted by Hermann Beckh

From Saint Patrick's Breastplate

Christ be with me, Christ within me,
  Christ behind me, Christ before me,
Christ beside me, Christ to win me,
  Christ to comfort and restore me,
Christ beneath me, Christ above me,
  Christ in quiet, Christ in danger,
Christ in hearts of all that love me,
  Christ in mouth of friend and stranger.

A Christmas Prayer

Come, Child, into our hearts, and still the storm
That our lone selfhood has let wrestle there;
And weave again the fabric of mankind
Out of Thy Light, Thy Life, Thy loving Fire.

Adam Bittleston

For Strength

The soul's longings are like seeds,
Out of which deeds of will are growing
And life's fruits are ripening

I can feel my destiny and my destiny finds me.
I can feel my star and my star finds me.
I can feel my aims and my aims are finding me.
The World and my soul are one great unity.

Life grows brighter around me
Life becomes harder for me
Life will be richer within me.

Rudolf Steiner

That the Good Will of God may be Fulfilled

Grant me, O most merciful Jesus, Thy grace, that it may be with me, and labour with me, and abide with me even to the end.

Give me grace ever to desire and to will what is most acceptable to Thee, and most pleasing in Thy sight. Let Thy Will be mine, and let my will ever follow Thine, and fully accord with it.

Let there be between Thee and me but one will, so that I may love what Thou lovest and abhor what Thou hatest; and let me not be able to will anything which Thou dost not will, nor to dislike anything which Thou dost will.

Grant that I may die to all things which are on the earth, and for Thy sake love to be despised, and to be unknown in the world.

Grant to me, above all things to be desired, that I may rest in Thee, and that my heart may find its peace in Thee. Thou art the peace of my heart, Thou its sole repose; out of Thee all things are hard and unquiet.

In this very peace, that is in Thyself, the sole, the supreme, the eternal Good, I will sleep and take my rest.

Thomas à Kempis

Lord, make me an instrument of Thy peace;
Where there is hatred, let me sow love;
Where there is injury, pardon;
Where there is discord, union;
Where there is doubt, faith;
Where there is despair, hope;
Where there is darkness, light;
Where there is sadness, joy.

O Divine Master, grant that I may not so much seek
To be consoled, as to console;
To be understood, as to understand;
To be loved, as to love;
For it is in giving that we receive,
It is in pardoning that we are pardoned,
And it is in dying that we are born to Eternal Life.

St Francis

O Christ,
Grant me the power
That I may govern
Hands, and feet, and senses, and word.
Help me to use them
For right deeds and right ways,
For pure thoughts
And loving counsel.
Lead me,
So that I do not build errors into my being.
Warn me, that I should forgive
When someone has harmed me!
Then I shall build in such a way
That I will the Good
When I return.
Warn me, that I should repent
When I have caused someone pain.
Then I shall build in such a way
That I shall think the Truth
When I return.
Bestow it upon me, that I share the joy
And the sufferings of others,
That I become a fellow creator
In harmony with each one's ways.

Albert Steffen

O Word of Waters
Be born on my lips;
So may I be Thy Word.

O Gift of Fire
Be born in my heart:
So may I be Thy Gift.

O Bread of the Earth
Be born in my hands;
So may I be Thy Food.

Leo Baker

A Meditation

Light in the world —
World in the mind —
Mind in the heart —

Pain in the day —
Strength in the pain —
Light in the strength —
World in the light.

Owen Barfield

St Bride's Song

Christ! King of the elements,
    Hear me.
Earth, bear me.
Air, lift me.
Fire, cleanse me.
Water, quicken me.

Christ! King of the elements,
    Hear me.
I will bear the burden of the earth with Thee.
I will lift my heart through the air to Thee.
I will cleanse my desire for love of Thee.
I will offer my life renewed to Thee.

Christ, King of the elements!
Water, fire, air and earth:
Weave within my heart this day
A cradle for Thy birth.

Andrew Keith

Blessing

May the road rise to meet you,
May the wind be always at your back.
May the sun shine warm upon your face,
The rain fall soft upon your fields,
And until we meet again
May God hold you in the palm of His hand.

Irish

A Birthday Song

The sun in your heart shall glow
The stars round your head shall sound,
The moon shall uphold from below
The earth shall give firm ground

Holding up high your head
Stretching your hands out wide
Your feet surely tread
With the Grace of God to guide

Evelyn Capel

Prayer to the Hierarchies

O Angels, who reveal to the spiritual soul
    Christ's spiritualizing of the seven planets;
O Archangels, who teach human hearts to understand
    each other's speech
    bringing about fellowship of the Holy Spirit;
O Archai, who dower the minds of men
    with creative thoughts
    and work in upon the earth
    from encircling spirit-spaces;
O Exousiai, who harmonize through sound
    who gave yourselves for garment
    for the incarnating world
O Dynameis, who drew man's soul from the starry heaven
    and from the starry heavens
    still ray down your forces
    to the earth
O Kyriotetes, who brought mankind the sun-gift
    of the life-body whose dominion
    lies in the pure working of God's will;
O Thrones, who poured out your own fire
    to be the substance of Saturn,
    and in the sacrifice became creating gods
O Cherubim, who dwell in the high brightness
    whose shadow is our air
    who at the gate of the lost Eden
    point with flaming sword to Christ's New City
O Seraphim, in whom love is so swift
    that in the seeing of God's thought
    it is wrought already;

O Michael, you who lead the heavenly hosts
    against the dragon
    and rule the realm of the stars
    as Regent of Christ;
O Gabriel, you who bring the tidings
    of descending souls,
    and on whom the cloven flame
    of Pentecost already rests;
O Raphael, Archangel of Spring,
    of Easter and of healing,
    Archangel of unfallen and redemptive life-forces;
May we learn to know you in your true forms
    and workings,
May we strive to shape our impulses
    to the pattern of your workings,
That on your wings, inwoven with our human nature,
    we may be borne
To be builders and citizens of Christ's New Earth.

Isobel Wyatt

For a Midsummer Fire

Flames flow upward
Smoke spread outward
Ash drop downward
Fire transmuting
Smoke dissolving
Ash deadening.
Flames of Spirit spring
Heavenward from human hearts.
Smoke of darkness dissolve
Into nought from human souls.
Ashes of death lie quiet —
Seed-bed of Spirit in human forms.

Evelyn Capel

St John's Tide

In the brightness,
in the magnificence of power
shining in the sun,
the warning sounds;
turn from the outer to the inner,
set the heart alight
with the flame of burning zeal
that He who comes
be seen and known,
light-sender,
love-giver.

Evelyn Capel

Michaelmas

The sword-wielder,
the dragon-confronter,
gathering up the true aims,
shielding the purposes of our hearts.
He watches over the conflicts
of the dark time,
sending down iron courage
from the shooting stars,
lifting the heart to see ahead
the light that overcomes in darkness.

Evelyn Capel

Christmas

I went walking under a cloud.
The cloud was thick above my head.
What is beyond the cloud? I said.

I went asking from day to day
what sounds were those from out of sight?
Angels are gathering in the light.

Some came running to Bethlehem,
the Heavens had opened to their sight.
Angels proclaimed the coming light.

Some went riding to Bethlehem,
the star went gliding overhead.
The light will shine on earth, they said.

I was obscured within the cloud.
Is the light lost to me? I cried.
It shines within, angels replied.

I parted the cloud and folded it.
A cloak it seemed to clothe the light.
Within the cloud the glow gleams bright.

Evelyn Capel

Worship

In thinking about the Act of Consecration of Man one can say to oneself:

I am a being of Spirit, an eternal soul living in a world of ordinary things. I approach the altar and become aware of the eternal spirit in me. The candles lit on the altar tell me that I am at the threshold of the spiritual world. Here I meet Christ. The spiritual being in me, my ego, is releasing itself from my ordinary person and is going to meet the Son-God, the Father-God, through the power of the Spirit. At the end of the Act of Consecration of Man I shall carry into my ordinary life the light within which it will be renewed here by the light of Christ shining at the threshold.

Evelyn Capel

Prayer to the Father

Father, Thou who wast, art and shalt be,
In our very inmost being,
Thy Being is glorified in us all
    and highly praised.
Thy Kingdom expands itself in our deeds
    and in the conduct of our lives.
Thy Will we perform in the activity of our lives
As Thou, O Father, in our inmost hast laid it.
The food of Spirit, the Bread of life
Thou offerest us in superabundance
In all the changing conditions of our lives.
Let our compassion for others
    be a compensation for the guilt
    to which we succumb within us.
Let not the Tempter work
    in us beyond our strength:
For in Thy Being no temptation can persist,
For the Tempter is but illusion and deception,
    out of which Thou, O Father, leadest us,
    through the light of thy knowledge.
Thy power and majesty work in us
In all cycles of time.
    Amen.

Rudolf Steiner

Acknowledgements

The publisher wishes to thank the following authors and translators for permission to quote their verses:

Sibylle Alexander pp. 17, 46 (second), 64, 66 (second) 70, 71, 77; Peter Allan p. 35; Muriel Allen, p. 51; The *Christian Community Journal* for Adam Bittleston's Introduction, pp. 9–14, and for p. 63 (second); Andrew Dakers Ltd, London for p. 47 from *Stars, Roundelay* by Isobel Wyatt; Stanley Drake pp. 59 (both), 63 (first); Roger Druitt p. 60 (second); The *Golden Blade* for Owen Barfield p. 82; Eileen Hersey p. 54 Richard Lewis pp. 18, 20 (middle), 24, 25, 29, 31 (first), 74; Donald Perkins pp. 60 (first), 61 (second); Verlag für schöne Wissenschaften, Dornach for p. 80; Rudolf Steiner Press, London for pp. 16, 27, 28, 30 (second), 31 (second), 32, 36, 46 (first) from *Prayers for Mother and Children*, for pp. 33, 34 from *The Key of the Kingdom*, for p. 72 (second) from *Guidance in Esoteric Training*; Rudolf Steiner Publications, New York, for pp. 20 (first), 30 (first) from *The Portal of Initiation*; Isobel Wyatt, pp. 86–87.

While every effort has been made to trace the original author (and translator) this has not always been possible, and the publisher wishes to apologise in advance for any errors or omissions.